to my friend,

by Freya Winters

this book is for:

_____

introduction:

if you're reading this page, it's highly likely it's because you've been gifted this book by someone who holds you in the highest regard.

the words in this book have been carefully chosen to convey the deep love, gratitude, and admiration i have for you, my dear friend.

throughout the journey of our lives, you've played an irreplaceable role, and i want you to know how grateful i am for your presence.

though words may sometimes fall short, i hope these pages serve as a heartfelt testament to the significance you hold in my life.

as you turn each page, may you discover heartwarming messages crafted to bring a smile to your face and warmth to your heart.

i offer this gift to you with an abundance of love that words cannot fully capture, and i sincerely hope that the sentiments within resonate deeply with you.

with all my love,

....

to my friend - freya winters

DAY 1

the thing about our friendship is that there's no
jealousy—only praise, encouragement, and mutual
pride in each other. there's no competition;
we thrive both individually and together. we
complement each other so well. the safe space we've
created together is unmatched, and i'm proud of us
for nurturing such a beautiful friendship.

here's to our future together.

to my friend - freya winters

DAY 2

keep on thriving and striving through this life with that beautiful pure heart of yours. the positive impact you make on other people's lives just by existing is second to none. trust me, i've seen it with my own eyes.

you should be *so* proud of who you are.

to my friend - freya winters

DAY 3

if you ever have any doubts, remember that i'm right here cheering you on, always. i have no doubt in my mind that i am in fact your biggest fan, and that you will manifest everything you dream of one day. i just know it. you're powerful, you're resilient, and you're truly destined for greatness. watching you blossom is an absolute *dream*.

to my friend - freya winters

DAY 4

the truth is,

you've touched the parts of my soul i
thought no one could ever reach.

to my friend - freya winters

DAY 5

thank you for never making me feel like i'm just being tolerated.
thank you for making me feel welcome in every situation you
bring me into. thank you for standing by me, even when i'm
not around. thank you for advocating for me. thank you for
accepting me on my good days and on the days when the world
overwhelms me. thank you for giving me the space i need to
breathe, grow, and flourish into who i know i can become. thank
you for showing me that i truly light up a room when i walk
into it. thank you for showing me kindness when i could barely
show it to myself. thank you for showing me that i'm worthy of
everything beautiful this world has to offer.

thank you for everything.

to my friend - freya winters

DAY 6

i know you already know this, but:

you can talk to me about anything, absolutely anything, whenever you need to. nothing is off-limits, and i'll do everything i can to be whoever you need in that moment. i promise to keep your secrets safe and always have your best interests at heart.

i've got your back, always and *forever.*

to my friend - freya winters

DAY 7

you weren't put on this planet to be subtle, to be
dismissed, or to be silenced. you're here to experience
being human in whatever way that means for you.
don't let societal expectations divert you from the
direction you want to go.

to my friend - freya winters

DAY 8

at this point, you're more than a friend... (and not in a weird way). you're family. you're a part of my heart, my life, and my soul. you're a part of my future, my goals, and my dreams. i see us in everything that i do. our connection isn't one to be undermined.

i love our bond.

to my friend - freya winters

DAY 9

whenever you start to feel those familiar, unrelenting moments of overwhelm, remind yourself that you don't have to have it all figured out right now. you really don't. there's no rush. never rush the things that you crave deep in your soul. give your mind a breather, and give yourself a break. you're doing fine. you're doing more than fine, you're absolutely smashing life right now, you just can't see it because you're so focused on what you're *not* doing. you owe it to yourself to have more faith in your journey.

to my friend - freya winters

DAY 10

i'm a firm believer in souls not meeting by accident.
this friendship was *supposed* to happen. written in the
stars, as they say. we were always meant to take on the
world, side by side, experiencing incredible things and
laughing until it genuinely hurts.

this friendship is fate. i'm sure of it.

to my friend - freya winters

DAY 11

i hope you never forget that you deserve to be the
love of your own life.

you are worthy of unconditional love, kindness, and
compassion, and the first person who should give it
to you, is yourself.

to my friend - freya winters

DAY 12

since you came into my life, i've noticed that i laugh so
much more than before. whenever we part ways after
spending time together, i have a huge smile on my face
for the rest of the day. knowing that you're there for me
brings a peace i've never felt before. thank you for making
everything a little bit brighter.

life is wonderful when you're around.

to my friend - freya winters

DAY 13

one of the things i cherish most about our
friendship is how much fun we have together.
with you, the ordinary becomes extraordinary.

we could spend a day in a trash can and i have
no doubt we'd still have a hilarious time.

to my friend - freya winters

DAY 14

this year is your year. i just know it. it feels *different.*
all of this work you've been putting into yourself is about
to come to fruition. i don't know anyone who does it
quite like you. i hope you're proud of yourself, right down
to your core. things are about to get incomprehensibly
better.

..and if they don't—i'll be having a word with whoever's in
charge, because i'll accept no less than for you
to absolutely *thrive.*

DAY 15

the truth is, you've helped me through some of my darkest
times. in the moments when i lacked any sort of hope
or happiness, you were there. you were the only person
who waited patiently by my side, holding my hand and
promising me that things really would get better. and
guess what? they did.

without you, i wouldn't have had that hope to hold on to.
you have no idea how much of a positive impact you've
made on my life.

thank you just doesn't feel like enough.

to my friend - freya winters

DAY 16

repeat these affirmations today:

i have everything i need within my soul.
my dreams are worth dreaming and believing in.
i have an infinite amount of reasons to smile.
wealth is continuously seeking to fulfill me.
my success and happiness are inevitable.
i am lucky. i am a winner.
my soul is *glowing*.

to my friend - freya winters

DAY 17

no-one could *ever* replace you.

to my friend - freya winters

DAY 18

bad days are an inevitable part of a really good life.
even the people who seem to have it all together
experience bad days. don't let anyone fool you.

a bad day doesn't define your life.

to my friend - freya winters

DAY 19

i want you to know that you never owe me *anything*.
there are no expectations or unsaid obligations.
there's never any keeping score or holding each other
to unrealistic standards. this is a true, real, authentic
bond, and there's no space for any toxicity. let's
promise to be open, honest, and trusting with one
another always. our friendship is healthy and will
continue to thrive when we put in the work.

i love us.

to my friend - freya winters

DAY 20

walk in power toward the accomplishment of those
fabulous dreams of yours. don't get distracted on the
way. don't procrastinate over the things that don't
matter. tunnel vision right to the very end, my friend.
you're so close now. hold onto that passion and
thrive. all of this work will be worth it, i promise.

DAY 21

picture this:

it's 10 years from now, and we've both achieved everything we set out to do... and then some. we've surpassed our wildest expectations and grown in ways that even surprised us. each of us has a beautiful home that perfectly reflects our personalities—warm, cozy, filled with light, and brimming with love. sitting together in the sunshine, we're planning our next epic holiday. we celebrate our victories often, supporting each other through thick and thin, navigating paths that unveil amazing opportunities we never imagined.

we worked tirelessly to nurture a healthy, loving, and profound friendship that has blossomed beyond our dreams.

we did it. we made it. we weathered tough times and emerged stronger than ever.

and the best part? we did it together. here's to our incredibly bright future.

we've got this.

to my friend - freya winters

DAY 22

i hope that i have been even half as
good a friend as you have been for me.

DAY 23

be intentional with your feelings. choose and
prioritize the things that bring joy to your
heart. don't postpone your happiness due to
procrastination. act now and experience it.

you deserve to embrace positivity in
every aspect of your life.

to my friend - freya winters

DAY 24

to say you've changed my life
would be an understatement.

there are no words that can truly express how deeply
grateful i am to have crossed paths with you.

to my friend - freya winters

DAY 25

i just want you to remember that one day, although it
might not seem like it right now, you'll wake up, and that
burden you've been carrying for so long will have vanished.
those worries that cloud your mind and heart will
dissipate, and you'll be able to truly breathe. whatever it is
you're going through right now, it isn't forever.

don't let your brain trick you into thinking that
you'll never find peace again.

to my friend - freya winters

DAY 26

you're the first person i've been able to truly resonate
with. it's rare to find someone who wants more than
superficial, shallow connections, and the fact i've
been able to find you amongst all of the time wasters
and fakeness feels incredibly special.

i will protect this connection with my *life*.

DAY 27

do it for your inner child. do it for the little version
of you who deserved love, tenderness, and kindness.
do it for the little version of you whose dreams were
so big they were almost unimaginable. do it for the
little version of you who is desperate to see you
achieve greatness.

to my friend - freya winters

DAY 28

friend, thank you for...

checking in on me regularly.
making me laugh (those proper, belly laughs).
being an active listener and for always seeking to understand.
celebrating wins with me, big and small.
respecting my personal space.
the big deep chats. yes, those ones.
the comfortable silences with zero expectation.
finishing my sentences (we're so in sync).
allowing me to know what it feels like to trust and be trusted.
showing me what true, healthy friendship should really be like.

thank you for being the best person i've ever met.

to my friend - freya winters

DAY 29

this friendship is a connection that we can't explain.
it defies words. it is something only felt in the depths of our
souls, a bond that transcends any understanding.

i love it *so* much.

to my friend - freya winters

DAY 30

i hope that we remain friends until we're both old and grey. i
hope that if we ever have misunderstandings, we will always
pick up the phone to resolve them. i hope that we always strive
to understand and forgive, and move forward in our friendship
with patience and unconditional love. i hope we can plan
beautiful holidays when we're rich. i hope we have a future
filled with tears shed from laughing at silly situations.

i hope we have everything we ever wanted and more.

to my friend - freya winters

DAY 31

guess what? i won the friend lottery. me. i won.
you're the epitome of friendship. no one is better than
you. no doubt in my mind. you're the best of the best.

to my friend - freya winters

DAY 32

so many (and i mean so, so many) of
my favorite memories are with you.

we could write a whole book *full* of our escapades.

to my friend - freya winters

DAY 33

i just want to remind you that you have an infinite amount of reasons to be happy. the main one being that you're you - someone who i look up to, admire, and have a deep respect for. you inspire the people around you more than you'll ever be able to comprehend.

you're an absolute *star*.

to my friend - freya winters

DAY 34

this friendship is so good. it's almost a little bit too good. i haven't been able to find anyone who comes close to connecting with me like you do.

the bar has been set way too high.

to my friend - freya winters

DAY 35

please never forget that there is a huge hug waiting
right here for you whenever you may need it.

to my friend - freya winters

DAY 36

you deserve a love that feels like an eternal summer.
you deserve a love that wraps around you so gently
you barely notice the impact, but recognize how
pure it is. you deserve a love that makes you laugh
when all you want to do is cry. you deserve a
love that celebrates your wins and pushes you to
accomplish your goals. you deserve a love that kisses
the tears of happiness away. you deserve a love that
makes you feel safe and at *home*.

to my friend - freya winters

DAY 37

repeat these affirmations:

everything is happening just as it should.
i am fully aligned with my purpose and intentions.
i am drawn to goodness. positive energy seeks me out, always.
i am endlessly grateful for the air that fills my lungs.
i choose to trust the process.

to my friend - freya winters

DAY 38

the thing about you is, you walk through life with your head
held high. you don't let the little things get you down. you
exude confidence, inner peace, and an open mind. your
strength and tenacity are truly admirable. your heart is
pure, warm, and compassionate. you're a huge inspiration to
everyone around you, even if you may not realize it.

everyone should be a little more like you.

DAY 39

so much goodness is coming our way. i can feel it in my bones, from my head right down to the tips of my toes. we have so much to look forward to, even though we may not know exactly what that is yet. this month is our month. this year is our year. this life is our life. let's open our hearts to the abundance that is knocking on the door right now and let. it. in.

i'm excited. are you?

to my friend - freya winters

DAY 40

do you want to know what i absolutely live for?

locking eyes with you, knowing we just had
the exact same thought.
the uncontrollable giggles when we really
shouldn't be laughing (at all).
getting those "i've got some juicy gossip" messages.
going on road trips and singing our favorite
songs with the windows down.
having cozy evenings in, sending each other stupid
videos that no one else would find funny.
telling each other secrets that will never see
the light of day anywhere else.
being there for each other in moments
when no one else would.
growing together, in friendship and in life.

this is the type of friendship that makes
everything better.

forever grateful for you.

to my friend - freya winters

DAY 41

there's nothing i want more than to
laugh with you for the rest of my days.

to my friend - freya winters

DAY 42

you've weathered too many storms to give time to
those negative seeds of doubt in your mind. you've
been through way too much to criticize every aspect
of who you are. you're way too important to close your
eyes to the potential that sits before you.

to my friend - freya winters

DAY 43

let's embrace the quiet together, lost in the pages
of our books. let's journey into fantastical realms
and contemplate alternate realities, sharing in the
richness of our thoughts and imaginations. let's bond
over different characters and their lives, seeking to
find similarities in our own journeys and experiences.

to my friend - freya winters

DAY 44

promise me one thing:

that you'll never let fear make *any* decisions on your behalf.

to my friend - freya winters

DAY 45

just by taking one look at you, people can tell you
have a beautiful heart. your soul radiates warmth and
kindness, and you can feel it from a mile away.

you are literal *sunshine*.

to my friend - freya winters

DAY 46

your happiness is my top priority. i'm committed to being the best friend i can possibly be for you, no matter what.

to my friend - freya winters

DAY 47

even after all of the years we have known each other,
you are still the only person to make me laugh like that.

to my friend - freya winters

DAY 48

so much has changed in the time that we have been
connected. from significant personal milestones
to global events shaping our world, we've seen it
all together. life is crazy. it's incomprehensible.
nonsensical. but one thing that i know to be true is
that our friendship is one constant that i can have
continuous faith in. it will only deepen, grow, and
evolve into something even more beautiful.

to my friend - freya winters

DAY 49

the day you read this page, promise me this: you'll
do one thing today, big or small, that your future
self will absolutely love you for. do it. don't hesitate.

to my friend - freya winters

DAY 50

our friendship is just like the sun and the moon,
forever complementing each other perfectly. our
bond will continue to illuminate our lives just as the
sun does, while the moon provides its reassuring,
calming presence, offering peace, understanding, and
comfort during those darker periods. you are the sun,
and i am the moon. this friendship is *eternal*.

to my friend - freya winters

DAY 51

the first day we met, i had a feeling that we had something special. we clicked instantly. it didn't feel weird, uncomfortable, or unnatural; it just felt *right*. it was like two missing pieces finally finding each other in a puzzle. from that moment, i knew our connection was meant to be, destined to grow into something life-changing.

to my friend - freya winters

DAY 52

thank you for the tough love. i really mean it. i appreciate
the times when you've told me what i really didn't want
to hear but desperately needed to. being friends with
you has taught me how to create and stand by strong
boundaries. it has taught me how to recognize and avoid
those displaying inexcusable red flags. it has taught me
to dream big and achieve even better. most importantly,
it has taught me that i'm worthy of unconditional love—
from myself and the people around me. this friendship
has taught me more than i could ever write in one book,
and i honestly couldn't be more blessed.

DAY 53

i don't know exactly how you'll be feeling as
you read these words, but i sincerely hope that
something beautiful happens to you today. you
deserve an abundance of extraordinary happenings.

to my friend - freya winters

DAY 54

you're one of those people who make life
better just by simply existing. your presence
lights up any room you walk into, and your
soul inspires the people around you.

you're *unreal.*

to my friend - freya winters

DAY 55

nothing is ever awkward with us, and i mean *nothing*.
i adore the fact that we can be ourselves and talk about
anything, and not only that, but we can do it comfortably.

that's how i know this bond is truly something really special.

to my friend - freya winters

DAY 56

i just want you to know that there's no pressure with me.
i'm a low-maintenance friend with a lot of love, care, and
appreciation. i will always respect your space, honor your
boundaries, and i'll laugh with you until our sides hurt.
i'll be right by your side whenever you need me, and i'll
continue to be your friend for as long as you'll have me.

to my friend - freya winters

DAY 57

whatever path you end up taking, wherever the world takes you, i need you to know that i will always be here for you. i want to hear about your adventures. i want to laugh at your bad jokes. i want to see you absolutely flourish into the person i always knew you would be. i'm so proud of you.

i can't wait to see what life has in store for you.

to my friend - freya winters

DAY 58

meeting you felt like finding a song after years of trying to remember what it's called. it felt familiar, right. there was a you-shaped hole in all of those years, and i no longer feel lost.

i'm so happy to say that i finally found my soul-friend.

to my friend - freya winters

DAY 59

you really are one of the very few people in the world who understands me. i can't maintain a poker face when we're together; i know you'll see right through it the moment you lay eyes on me.

i know it's cliché, but it's true:
sometimes i think you know me better than i know myself.

to my friend - freya winters

DAY 60

it doesn't matter how late it is, how far apart
we are, or how long we've gone without
speaking, i am always here. i don't care what the
circumstances are—you can always call me, text
me, or show up at my house in the pouring rain.
i've got you.

to my friend - freya winters

DAY 61

being around you recharges me.
your energy is uplifting and invigorating—a true force for good.

to my friend - freya winters

DAY 62

i hold so much of you in my heart. whenever
you accomplish something, i feel it in my bones.
whenever you hurt, i feel it in my soul. whenever you
laugh, my spirit lifts with yours.

your happiness is my happiness.

to my friend - freya winters

DAY 63

what's the absolute best that could happen? what would completely blow your mind and rock your world, in the best way possible? what if everything worked out better than you could've ever imagined?

what if, everything actually was ok?

to my friend - freya winters

DAY 64

best friend, i really like the people we're becoming. i love us for the work we've put into bettering ourselves and improving our lives. i'm so proud of us for sticking with it and accomplishing so much more than we initially set out to do. i'm relieved that we're falling back in love with life again. it feels so good to finally be able to take a breath. we're doing an amazing job of living right now.

let's keep smashing it.

to my friend - freya winters

DAY 65

i'd choose you to be my best friend in every single plane of existence. you know when you find that one song that hits just right? when you find the restaurant that cooks your favorite meal the exact way you want it? when everything falls into place perfectly? that's what i've found with you.

it really doesn't get much better than this.

to my friend - freya winters

DAY 66

repeat these affirmations:

i am worthy. i am enough.
i always was, and i always will be.
i am proud of the person i am,
and who i'm growing to become.
my emotional state is balanced.
my mind is clear from all noise.
my heart is open to growth and *unconditional* love.

to my friend - freya winters

DAY 67

there is an endless amount of love to be found in every single corner of this friendship. everywhere i look when i think about us is just everything i've ever wanted. i'm so lucky.

to my friend - freya winters

DAY 68

not only are you my friend, but you're the friend i can
speak to about *anything*. you're the friend who will always
be up for a good time, rain or shine. you're the friend
who will listen to my ramblings when no one else will.
you're the friend who can make me laugh for hours on
end. you're the friend who continues to motivate me to
grow. you're the friend who would drive to me at 3 in
the morning if i needed a shoulder to cry on. you're the
friend who will always have my back in a room full of
haters. you're that friend. that friend i could rely on, no
matter what.

the only way i could ever thank you is to try and be the
friend to you that you have been to me.

to my friend - freya winters

DAY 69

you're the most down-to-earth, authentic, real, honest,
beautiful-hearted, abundant, trustworthy, fun-loving, exciting,
caring, and whole human i've ever encountered in this life.
i mean that from the bottom of my heart.

to my friend - freya winters

DAY 70

everything, and i mean *everything*
improved the second you entered my life.

to my friend - freya winters

DAY 71

there's nothing wrong with realizing you're a
little lost in this life, as long as you remember
that it's not forever.

it's never forever.

to my friend - freya winters

DAY 72

one of the main things i love about you is how
true to yourself you are. you're so authentically
you that no one could ever doubt your sincerity.
your authenticity will continue to pave the way
toward a beautiful future, and there's nothing i
want more than for you to live out your dreams.
keep on being effortlessly you.

to my friend - freya winters

DAY 73

thank you for never just disappearing, for not leaving when the going got tough. when i was in the midst of my suffering, you didn't go anywhere. at the time, i didn't know i was worthy of such care and kindness from another human. you raised the bar and lifted me up with you.

i'll *never* forget the things you've done for me.

to my friend - freya winters

DAY 74

you're the human definition of *sunshine*.

to my friend - freya winters

DAY 75

i wasn't even looking when i found you, and that's how i know
this friendship was meant to be. it was fate. letting life flow
and do its thing, slowly leading an unknowing me to you at
the right time... it was the best thing that could've happened.
perfect, divine timing. the gratitude i feel is beyond measure.

to my friend - freya winters

DAY 76

it's so hard to believe that at one point we were strangers.
we would have just walked past each other on the street, never
knowing that we could have a bond like this.

i wonder how different our lives would be?

to my friend - freya winters

DAY 77

i genuinely can't believe i'm lucky enough to have a friend that
i appreciate more and more every single day.

i've hit the friend jackpot ten times over with you.

to my friend - freya winters

DAY 78

forgive yourself for your shortcomings. don't hold
onto the mistakes you made while in survival mode.
never let guilt consume you; it benefits no one.
you're worthy of forgiveness, from others, but most
importantly from yourself. don't let yourself hold you
back; there's too much of this world to enjoy.

to my friend - freya winters

DAY 79

you and i, we've grown so much. and do you know
what the best part of that is? we've been lucky
enough to be with each other every single step of
the way. i love every single version of us we've been
over the years, and i simply cannot wait for the
growth that's to come.

to my friend - freya winters

DAY 80

i wish you could see yourself through my
eyes. maybe then you'd see what a powerful,
independent, open-minded, beautiful human
you really are. i'll be forever in awe of you.

to my friend - freya winters

DAY 81

thank you for allowing me to be myself when i'm around you.
you make my inner child the happiest they've ever been.

to my friend - freya winters

DAY 82

friends like you really are rare. i feel like i've been waiting
a lifetime to find someone i truly click with, can trust
completely, and can simply be comfortable doing nothing
with. our friendship is truly one in a million.

how lucky are we?

to my friend - freya winters

DAY 83

you're incredible. you can lift my spirits on my toughest days. you make me laugh at things that aren't even funny. you give me the motivation to get out of bed when i feel like the world is swallowing me up, and you inspire me to strive for more. thank you for showing me how to be a better person. you've made a huge impact on my life, in the best way possible.

to my friend - freya winters

DAY 84

thanks for being a real one. although it might have been tough to hear at the time, i'm so glad you haven't sugarcoated things when i've needed a reality check. having you bring me back down to earth during difficult times is something i'll be forever grateful for.

your tough love has been *invaluable*.

to my friend - freya winters

DAY 85

the thing about you is, you just make life *better*. i don't know how you do it. you're unlike anyone else i've ever met. things feel much lighter when you're around. your energy is contagious, but in the best possible way. there's not much i love more in this life than the fact that i get to spend time with you and call you my friend. thank you for being so wonderful.

to my friend - freya winters

DAY 86

it will never matter how long we spend apart; our friendship
is so rock solid that when we're next in each other's company,
it's like absolutely nothing has changed. it could be months,
years, a millennium...

this bond is unbreakable.
i wouldn't have it any other way.

to my friend - freya winters

DAY 87

your friendship genuinely means everything to me.

to my friend - freya winters

DAY 88

thank you for accepting me for who i am
at my core. thank you for letting me be
myself around you with no judgment, and
thank you for being the best friend anyone
could ever ask for.

to my friend - freya winters

DAY 89

you've been such a powerful constant over the years.
as life has ebbed and flowed, pulling me in different
directions and occasionally throwing me off course, you've
consistently realigned me and reminded me of my purpose.
without you, i think i'd be lost - and if i were, i just *know* i'd
find my way back to you again.

to my friend - freya winters

DAY 90

friend, let's grow together. let's heal together. let's experience
the world in all of its weird and wonderful ways. let's laugh
at things that simply aren't funny (to literally anyone else but
us) again and again and again. let's watch terrible movies and
adopt the best characters as our new personalities for the next
day, get bored, and do it all over again. let's dream together.
let's trust each other. let's enjoy life together. i love nothing
more in this world than doing life with you.

to my friend - freya winters

DAY 91

the truth is, there isn't enough space in my heart,
or words in my mind to express how much i truly
appreciate you. nothing will *ever* do it justice.

to my friend - freya winters

DAY 92

thank you for all of the time you've spent being my
shoulder to cry on, reassuring me that everything really
will be okay, and for giving me advice that maybe i didn't
want to hear but you knew i needed. thank you for being
such a solid and understanding friend. you're one of a
kind, and i mean that with every single fiber of my being.

to my friend - freya winters

DAY 93

this friendship embodies healthiness.
it has taught me invaluable lessons about love—how to give
it and receive it. our bond has reaffirmed my worthiness of
abundant respect and kindness, making it a non-negotiable
in my life.

my standards have been elevated, and it's all thanks to you.

to my friend - freya winters

DAY 94

you've proven to me that soulmates exist, and that they
aren't confined to lovers. they exist in the depths of platonic
connections, waiting to be unraveled. you're my soul friend, my
best friend, my favorite person ever to walk this earth.

to my friend - freya winters

DAY 95

this friendship took my hand and showed
me how to fall right back in love with life again.

to my friend - freya winters

DAY 96

i hope this chapter of your life feels really, really good. i hope that the months ahead are full of abundance, wealth, good health, opportunities, growth, and healing. i hope that your dreams come true, and when they do, they multiply into something you can't even comprehend right now.

DAY 97

i feel so lucky to be able to say that this is a friendship where we both grow. learn. adapt. evolve. *bloom.* we do all of this together, and for that, i'll be forever grateful.

having a friend like you is life-changing.

DAY 98

my favorite place in the world is
wherever i am when i'm with you.

to my friend - freya winters

DAY 99

promise me you'll *never* settle for any less than you deserve.

to my friend - freya winters

DAY 100

now that we've reached the end of this book, i
want you to truly understand how deeply loved
and cherished you are. your presence in my life
is immensely appreciated, and i'll never tire of
expressing my gratitude for our friendship. you've
become an integral part of my chosen family, and
no matter where our paths may lead, you will always
hold a special place in my heart.

i love you *endlessly*.

Made in the USA
Columbia, SC
18 November 2024

46939570R00064